CELEBRITY BIOS

Elijah Wood

Danny Fingeroth

HIGH
interest
books

Children's Press®
A Division of Scholastic Inc.
New York / Toronto / London / Auckland / Sydney
Mexico City / New Delhi / Hong Kong
Danbury, Connecticut

Book Design: Erica Clendening
Contributing Editor: Scott Waldman

Photo Credits: Cover © Fitzory Barrett/Globe Photos Inc.; p. 4
© DMI/TimePix; p. 7 © Lisa Rose/Globe Photos Inc.; pp. 8, 10 © Michael
Ferguson/Globe Photos Inc.; pp. 13, 14, 23, 28, 32 courtesy Everett
Collection; pp. 17, 19, 20, 31 © Globe Photos Inc.; p. 25 © Sonia
Moskowitz/Globe Photos Inc.; p. 26 © Robert Eric/Corbis Sygma; p. 34
© Tom Rodriguez/Globe Photos Inc.; p. 37 © Mitchell Gerber/Corbis; p. 39
© Roger Harvey/Globe Photos Inc.

Library of Congress Cataloging-in-Publication Data

Fingeroth, Danny.
    Elijah Wood / Danny Fingeroth.
      p. cm.—(Celebrity bios)
    Summary: Profiles Elijah Wood, the actor who stars as Frodo Baggins in
    the Lord of the Rings films.
    Includes bibliographical references and index.
    ISBN 0-516-24336-5 (lib. bdg.)—ISBN 0-516-27858-4 (pbk.)
    1. Wood, Elijah, 1981—Juvenile literature. 2. Motion picture actors
    and actresses—United States—Biography—Juvenile literature. [1. Wood,
    Elijah, 1981- 2. Actors and actresses.] I. Title. II. Series.

PN2287.W575F56 2003
791.43'028'092—dc21

                                                    2003000915

CONTENTS

CHAPTER ONE

The Journey Begins

"I grew up fast mentally and didn't relate to people my own age. They were focused on their next night's homework. I was concentrating on my lifelong career."

—Elijah in *YM Magazine*

Though he's quite young, Elijah Wood has built an amazing career. He started out as a child actor in a Paula Abdul video. He then moved on to small roles in *Back to the Future II* and *Internal Affairs*. Only a few years later, Elijah came into his own in Barry Levinson's film

While other boys his age were worried about things such as whether or not they would make the basketball team, Elijah focused on his career goals.

Avalon. From there, it's been one success after another. The crowning achievement of his career so far has been his performances in the *Lord of the Rings* trilogy. Let's take a closer look at one of Hollywood's hottest young stars.

CHILD OF THE MIDWEST

Elijah Jordan Wood was born January 28, 1981, in Cedar Rapids, Iowa. Elijah's parents gave all their children biblical names. Elijah's older brother is named Zachariah. His younger sister's name is Hannah. Elijah's parents owned a deli in Cedar Rapids. His mother was his main influence. His father didn't have much of a presence in his early life. "I was not raised by my dad," he told *Rolling Stone*. "He was always physically there as a father, but never emotionally there."

While Elijah is very close to the rest of his family, that doesn't mean everybody gets along

Elijah has always been very close with his family. In this 1997 photo, he's taking his younger sister Hannah to the premiere of *Titanic*.

all the time. "My mom and my sister are actually most alike," Elijah told *Rolling Stone*. "They have quite fiery personalities. When they get angry at each other, it's like an explosion. I try to talk things out. I was always the family peacemaker."

Elijah may have been the family peacemaker, but he was a bundle of energy, too. That's why Elijah was attracted to acting at an early age. He needed to do something to burn off all that extra energy. Elijah loved climbing things. His family and friends called him Sparkplug and Monkey. When he was

As a child actor, Elijah made enough money to support his family.

two, he locked his mother out of the house. Then, he climbed into the cupboards and made a huge mess in the kitchen while she watched from outside!

CALIFORNIA, HERE I COME!

One day, while watching television, Elijah's mother came up with a way to channel her son's extra energy into something positive. *Elijah could work as a child actor in commercials*, she thought. She enrolled him in a local modeling school when he was six years old. Soon afterward, a talent agent spotted him. The agent asked Elijah if he wanted to act. Of course he did! Elijah, along with his mother, brother, and sister moved to Los Angeles. Elijah's father soon joined them there. The journey west proved to be the biggest—and best—move in young Elijah's life.

CHAPTER TWO

New Kid in Town

"I think there's a good chance Elijah will be like a Ron Howard. He's smart and he's interested, and he has a sense of where the scene should be. And he's naturally bossy."

—Director Joseph Rubin in
Entertainment Weekly

LIFE IN LOS ANGELES

Once Elijah arrived in Los Angeles, he took only six weeks to start working. He was cast in Paula Abdul's 1989 "Forever Your Girl" video. The video was directed by David Fincher.

Even as a young boy, Elijah was a natural actor.

Fincher went on to direct *Seven*, *Fight Club*, and *Panic Room*.

After "Forever Your Girl," Elijah appeared in *Back to the Future II*. His part was so small that he was simply listed as "Video Game Boy" in the credits. Elijah also had a small role in 1990's *Internal Affairs*. He played an innocent but smart kid. Since Elijah was so young and was just starting as an actor, he didn't have very many lines. Although Elijah was never trained in acting, he was showing a talent that directors were beginning to notice. Once he

Did you know?

By the time Elijah costarred in *The War* with Kevin Costner, he was so popular his name received equal billing with Costner's on the posters advertising the movie.

In *Avalon*, Elijah proved he could be a serious actor,
capable of handling a major role in a film.

got started, he found he definitely had a knack
for the big screen.

Elijah's first major role came in 1990 when
he was cast in *Avalon*. Barry Levinson was the
director. Being cast as the character of Michael
Kaye was a great honor because the movie was

Elijah played Huck Finn in 1993's *The Adventures of Huck Finn*. Courtney B. Vance played his friend. In the story, a mischievous boy and a slave run away and sail a homemade raft down a river.

based on Levinson's own life. Elijah's character was based on Levinson as a young boy.

In 1992, Elijah starred in *Radio Flyer*. In this movie, Elijah played Mike, a little boy with an abusive stepfather. Mike wants to build a wagon that can fly so he and his brother can escape from their house. Next came *The Witness*, a Showtime TV-series episode about the Holocaust.

In 1993's *The Adventures of Huck Finn*, Elijah made his mark as an actor, even though he wasn't a teenager yet. His costar Courtney B. Vance raved about Elijah in *YM*: "People had a tendency to treat Jah Jah (Vance's nickname for Elijah) as an adult because he was always so professional. But Deborah (Elijah's mom) was there for Elijah, keeping him balanced and making sure no one forgot he was an eleven-year-old." Also in 1993, Elijah played opposite Macauley Culkin in *The Good Son*.

Up to this time, Elijah had spent his career acting only in dramas. He wanted to prove he could do comedy, too. That chance soon came. Elijah starred in Rob Reiner's *North* in 1994.

In the film, he played North, an eleven-year-old boy who feels unappreciated by his parents. He files a lawsuit against them. North then sets off on a funny journey to find parents who really care about him.

In 1994, Elijah had another starring role in *The War*. This time he got to work with one of Hollywood's most respected actors, Kevin Costner. Once again, his performance earned him praise from the adults he worked with. "He's the first child actor I've worked with that I think is really an actor," *War* director Jon Avnet told *Entertainment Weekly*. "He's not tied to his cuteness."

While working in California, Elijah went to regular schools for a while. Then, due to his hectic acting schedule, he was homeschooled. Elijah was happier that way. However, when he was eleven years old, Elijah had some doubts about his career. Not being around other kids

Elijah faced many pressures as an actor. By the time he starred in 1994's *The War* with Lexi Randall (left) and Kevin Costner, he was actually thinking about quitting.

his age was hard. For a short time, he thought about quitting acting. Eventually, he changed his mind. He started enjoying acting more than he missed being in a normal school. Today, Elijah is especially glad that he didn't have to worry about issues such as whether or not he fit in with certain groups of kids.

Elijah was handling the difficult world of child acting very well. He knew that many young stars are never heard from again after their early successes. As Elijah got a little older, he reached a major turning point in his career. He was no longer a child. Could he graduate to older roles? Many child actors are unable to do so. Elijah, however, had great success with more mature roles. In 1997 and 1998, he appeared in *The Ice Storm*, *Deep Impact*, and *The Faculty*. Ang Lee was the director of *The Ice Storm*. Lee is also the director of the *Incredible Hulk* movie.

Director Robert Rodriguez, who worked with Elijah on *The Faculty* told *Gear* magazine, "Elijah can easily get people to see him differently. He's an internal actor, very strong."

The Faculty was yet another new step for Elijah. It was the first thriller he had appeared in.

Elijah has done television work, too. He appeared in an episode of *Homicide: Life on the Street*. His voice was also featured in an episode of *Frasier*.

In 2001, at age twenty, Elijah was on the fast track of Hollywood success- –and yet nothing could have prepared him for his next amazing film role.

CHAPTER THREE

The Making of a Superstar

"I did a lot of growing up; I probably aged ten years. The person who went to New Zealand and the person who left there are significantly different."

—Elijah in *YM* magazine

When Elijah was cast as Frodo Baggins in the *Lord of the Rings (LOTR)* movies, he went from being a recognized actor to one of Hollywood's hottest stars. Frodo is the main character in all three *LOTR* movies.

Elijah's acting career has been forever changed because of his role as Frodo Baggins.

ELIJAH WOOD

The *Lord of the Rings* is a movie trilogy based on books written by J.R.R. Tolkien. The books were published in 1954 and 1955. In them, Frodo the hobbit, a small humanlike creature, travels to a dark, evil place called Mordor. In Mordor, Frodo must destroy a magic ring by throwing it into the fires of Mount Doom, a volcano. Battling against Frodo is Sauron, the Dark Lord, to whom the ring once belonged. If Frodo fails, evil will take over the whole world.

To earn the role of Frodo, Elijah made his own audition tape. He wanted to show that he was the right actor for the job. Elijah hired a voice coach so that he could work on a special

Did you know?

Tolkien published his first book about hobbits in 1937. He spent the next seventeen years working on the *Lord of the Rings* trilogy.

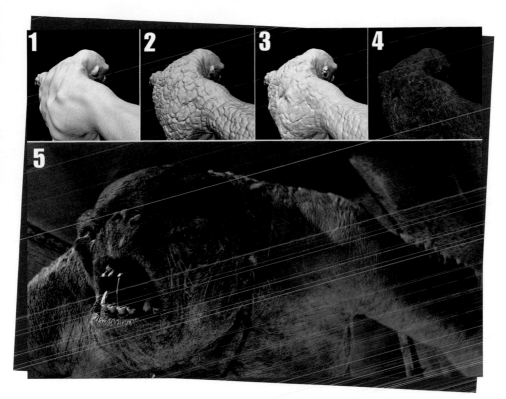

After Elijah finished filming his parts in *LOTR,* computer specialists went in and added additional characters and landscapes. The monster in frame 5 was created on a computer by adding the layers shown in frames 1 through 4.

accent. He and his friends rented fancy costumes. Even though it was only an audition tape, they shot the scenes as if they were part of a real film. Each scene was shot using different angles. Elijah and his friends then edited the footage. The next day Elijah brought the video to the movie's casting office.

ELIJAH WOOD

The video audition was a hit. Elijah got the role. He also got himself into one of the most difficult movie shoots of all time. Director Peter Jackson took the cast and crew to New Zealand. There, they shot all three *LOTR* movies at once. They worked on the movies for sixteen difficult months.

Like Elijah, everyone who worked on *LOTR* loved the project. However, they all agreed it was the hardest movie they had ever worked on. As Elijah told *Newsweek*: "It was so much more amazing than it was difficult. But…it was one of the most difficult experiences of my life. I've never felt so tired in my life. The things that were asked of us…were really extreme. But at the end of the day, it didn't matter. We were so passionate about what we were a part of."

The cast of the trilogy became great friends. Elijah and Sean Astin, who played Sam Wise, became especially close. Elijah ran into Sean about four or five days before they had to go to New Zealand for the first time. They both happened to be walking through a hotel lobby at the same time. They recognized each other

Sir Ian McKellen played Gandolph in *LOTR*. He is such a highly respected actor in England that he was knighted by the queen.

Many fans of the *LOTR* trilogy were happy with the way director Peter Jackson (center) transformed their favorite books into films. They were also pleased with how the cast played the characters.

immediately. Both of them stopped in their tracks and just looked at each other for a second. Then they ran over and hugged. It was the first time they had ever met. Instantly, they connected as friends. They knew they were about to work on a very special project together.

Fans of the *LOTR* trilogy took the books very seriously. Elijah knew his performance as Frodo had to live up to their expectations. It was one of Elijah's greatest challenges in making the movie. Since the books were so famous, many people had different ideas as to how Frodo should act. As soon as the filming started though, Elijah began to feel comfortable with the choices he was making as an actor. He wasn't the only one either.

Director Peter Jackson was very happy with the way Elijah chose to play the role of Frodo. Elijah let the character of Frodo take over his actions. He just went along for the ride.

The first couple of months of filming were very difficult for Elijah. He got burned out very quickly from the long schedule. So Elijah took time away from the movie and went home for

Christmas. He spent his time off taking it easy. He loved being home because that was the first time he had relaxed in months. When he went back to New Zealand for more filming he never felt homesick again. After being away from New Zealand for so long, he realized he loved working there. His time at home had given him new strength and focus.

One of the hardest things about the role was wearing the makeup and costumes. Elijah wore fake feet and ears as well as lots of makeup every day. He had never dressed up like this for a part before. He was very impressed by the hard work of the makeup people and costume designers. Every morning they started at 5 A.M. He and the other actors had to stand for an hour and a half while their fake feet and ears were glued on.

FRIENDS FOREVER

One of the great things for Elijah about working on the trilogy was the connection he made with his costars. He got to work side by side with great actors such as Cate Blanchett, Liv Tyler, and Ian McKellen.

During the filming, many of the actors whose characters were friends in the movie became

Many film critics thought Elijah did a great job at expressing a wide range of emotions, such as fear and love, in *LOTR*.

friends in real life. For Elijah, that made the project much more enjoyable. His character's friendship with Sean Astin's character was much more authentic because of the young men's real-life friendship. Elijah made some of the best friends of his life while filming the movie.

"Because we were so close, and because we spent so much time together, I think showing that relationship was effortless," Elijah told *Scifi.com.* "It wasn't something we actually had to think about; it worked on its own because we were so close in real life and we knew so much about each other."

As a big movie fan himself, Elijah was thrilled to work with so many other famous actors. He was particularly excited to work with Ian McKellen, who played Gandolph; Ian Holm, who played Bilbo Baggins; and Christopher Lee, who played Saruman. The person he was most nervous to work with was

Cate Blanchett. Though they were only in a few scenes together, one of them was very long. Fortunately for Elijah, he was able to get over his anxiety and ended up doing a great job.

Elijah struggled the hardest during his scenes with Cate Blanchett. He was nervous because he considers her to be a great actress.

CHAPTER FOUR

Elijah Offscreen

"I like to chat with people and show them that I'm as normal as they are."

—Elijah in *Gear* magazine

Elijah enjoys his social life. He has dated several actresses, including Franka Potente, the star of *The Bourne Identity* and Elijah's costar in *Try Seventeen*. He also had a few relationships in New Zealand while filming *Lord of the Rings*. Right now, there's no one special in his life.

"I'm oddly insecure when it comes to women," he told *Gear* magazine. "It's kind of strange. I'm a really confident individual and I

Even though he's a highly successful actor and a millionaire, Elijah is still insecure around women.

ELIJAH WOOD

34

Did you know?

Elijah and eight of his costars in *Lord of the Rings* all got tattoos to remember their experience with the film. In the film, their characters made up the Fellowship of the Ring.

have a lot to offer." For Elijah, the ideal woman has a sense of humor and the ability to laugh. Elijah is very attracted to women who have self-confidence. "I really enjoy women who have a strong sense of themselves, who aren't afraid to speak their mind," Elijah told *YM*. That's not all. Elijah believes fully in romance. Any woman he dates must be able to appreciate something like a nice candlelight dinner.

Elijah, shown here with Salma Hayek, has dated a few actresses. He hasn't found the woman he wants to settle down with just yet, though.

THE MUSIC MAN

Acting is just one of Elijah's passions. The other thing he gets excited about is music. Elijah is a music fanatic. He loves just about all kinds of music. His favorite band is Smashing Pumpkins. When he went to see former Smashing Pumpkins leader Billy Corgan's new group, Zwan, he spent hours happily talking to other Pumpkins fans. They talked about the rare CDs and live recordings that they all owned. Elijah was quite comfortable being the *fan*, instead of the star.

Elijah loves music of all kinds. He plays DJ whenever he gets a chance. He became the DJ of choice at many parties the *LOTR* cast and crew held while in New Zealand. Elijah took about three hundred CDs with him to New Zealand. He bought another three hundred while he was there. A local bar let him be the DJ for several of its parties. Elijah absolutely loved the experience. Playing the music that

The Smashing Pumpkins is Elijah's favorite group. He has a large collection of rare Smashing Pumpkins recordings.

could make an entire room of people dance was a great thrill for the young actor. Elijah played lots of his favorite music. Some of his favorites that got a lot of airplay include the Beatles, Radiohead, Jimi Hendrix, Massive Attack, Propellerhead, Liquid Soul, John Lennon, and the Flaming Lips.

JUST A REGULAR GUY

Even though Elijah is now a big star, he doesn't forget that he's no different than everyone else. Elijah really gets a kick out of his fans. Once, on a flight from Los Angeles to Vancouver, three very young fans approached the actor. A flight attendant asked Elijah if she should send the kids back to their parents. Elijah told her he didn't mind the kids sitting with him at all. He spent the rest of the long trip letting them take turns sitting next to him. He signed autographs, played games, and told silly jokes.

Elijah is really appreciative of fans. Being so young and so famous can be difficult. People constantly stop Elijah and want to talk to him. For many, such fame can be a huge ego boost. However, his mom raised him to be down to earth. So when everyone in a restaurant turns around to look at him, Elijah doesn't let the attention go to his head.

For all his success, Elijah doesn't see himself as being any different from other guys his age. "I'm into girls, video games, and music," Elijah

Elijah has become rich and famous at an early age. However, he still acts like most young men in their early twenties: He spends his free time buying music or playing video games.

told *YM*. "See, I'm like any other guy my age." For one thing, he *still* lives with his mom.

Elijah has a separate guesthouse on the same property as his mom's house near Los Angeles. She still does his laundry. He's also still very close to his brother and sister. Zachariah produces video games in San Diego. He generally comes home every second weekend. Eighteen-year-old Hannah is a poet.

ON THE HORIZON

So what has this amazingly accomplished young man done recently and what's in his future?

Of course, there's the third installment of the *LOTR* trilogy, *The Return of the King*. Elijah is also starring in *Try Seventeen*, which was shot in Vancouver, British Columbia. That's not all Elijah has done since *LOTR*. He has already been in *Thumbsucker*. The movie is a drama directed by Mike Mills, based on a novel by Walter Kirn. Elijah plays Justin Cobb. Also starring in it are Tilda Swinton and Scarlett Johansson.

Elijah also finished the film *Ash Wednesday*. The film takes place in Manhattan in the early 1980s. In the film, two Irish American brothers run into trouble with some gangsters. Elijah plays one of the brothers, Sean Sullivan.

Edward Burns plays Francis Sullivan, the other brother. Elijah enjoyed working with Burns, who also directed the film. He had only good things to say about the experience. Elijah told *Interview Magazine*, "...I've got a lot of respect for his method of filmmaking. It's all about no frills and a little crew getting together and working at a fast pace."

Elijah is also providing the voice for Tom Thumb in the upcoming animated movie *The Adventures of Tom Thumb and Thumbelina*. The young actor is definitely keeping busy.

Many actors in Hollywood eventually want to direct their own movies. Elijah hasn't gotten that far yet, but he is thinking of writing some things for himself as an experiment. He likes to keep his options open, rather than be categorized as just an actor, director, or writer.

Elijah's future seems like it's going to be very exciting. Look at all he's done at such a young age. We can only imagine the success that the coming years will bring for him.

TIMELINE

1981
- Elijah Wood is born on January 28, in Cedar Rapids, Iowa.

1987
- Elijah is enrolled in modeling school at age six.
- After being spotted by a talent agent, Elijah moves to Los Angeles to work as an actor.

1989
- Paula Abdul releases her "Forever Your Girl" video, which features Elijah.
- Elijah has a small role in *Back to the Future II*.

1990
- *Internal Affairs* is released.
- Elijah has his first big film role in Barry Levinson's *Avalon*.

1992
- Elijah stars in *Radio Flyer*.
- Elijah also stars in *Witness*, a Holocaust drama on Showtime television.

1993
- Elijah appears in Disney's adaptation of *The Adventures of Huck Finn*.
- Macauley Culkin and Elijah star in *The Good Son*.

TIMELINE

1994
- Elijah receives top billing in Rob Reiner's outlandish comedy *North*.
- *The War*, with Elijah and Kevin Costner, is released.

1996
- Elijah returns to the big screen in a version of *Flipper*.

1997
- Ang Lee's *The Ice Storm* is released, starring Elijah.

1998
- Elijah moves into older roles in *Deep Impact* and *The Faculty*.

2001
- The first movie of the *Lord of the Rings* trilogy, *The Fellowship of The Ring*, is released.

2002
- The second *LOTR* movie, *The Two Towers*, is released.
- Elijah appears in *Ash Wednesday* and *Try Seventeen*.

2003
- The third *LOTR* movie, *The Return of the King*, is released.

Name	Elijah Jordan Wood
Born	January 28, 1981
Birthplace	Cedar Rapids, Iowa
Family	Mother, Debbie; father, Warren; brother, Zachariah; sister, Hannah
Nicknames	Lij, Eli, Monkey, Elwood, Fozzie
Height	5'7"
Hair	Brown
Eyes	Blue
Sign	Aquarius

Favorites

Hobbies	Fencing, photography, swimming, basketball, in-line skating, cooking, singing, playing hockey, video games, reading, collecting *Star Wars* memorabilia
Bands	Smashing Pumpkins, The Beatles, Radiohead, Jim Hendrix, Wilco
TV Shows	*Extra* and *Entertainment Tonight*
Movies	*Braveheart, Star Wars, Amelie, Mulholland Drive, Pulp Fiction, Heavenly Creatures*
Super Hero	Batman

abusive (uh-**byoos**-siv) treating a person or animal cruelly

accomplished (uh-**kom**-plisht) skillful

anxiety (ang-**zye**-uh-tee) a feeling of worry or fear

audition (aw-**dish**-uhn) a short performance by an actor to see whether he or she is suitable for a part in a play or movie

channel (**chan**-uhl) to aim a thing or a feeling in a certain direction or to a certain end

expectation (ek-spek-**tay**-shuhn) the state of expecting, or looking forward to

interpretation (in-tur-pri-**tay**-shuhn) a particular version of something

knack (**nak**) an ability to do something difficult or tricky

passionate (**pash**-uh-nit) having or showing very strong feelings

transition (tran-**zish**-uhn) a change from one form, condition, or place to another

FOR FURTHER READING

Degnen, Lisa. *Elijah Wood: Hollywood's Hottest Rising Star*. Boston, MA: Warner Books, 1999.

Sibley, Brian. *The Lord of the Rings: The Making of the Movie Trilogy*. New York: Houghton Mifflin, 2002.

Sibley, Brian. *The Lord of the Rings Official Movie Guide*. New York: Houghton Mifflin, 2001.

RESOURCES

WEB SITES

www.elijahfan.com/
This fan site links you to photos, news updates, and articles about Elijah.

http://us.imdb.com/Name?Wood,+Elijah
The Internet Movie Database is a source of information about any movie. Be sure to check it out to learn about Elijah's career.

INDEX

INDEX

ABOUT THE AUTHOR

Danny Fingeroth was the editor of Spider-Man comics at Marvel Comics for many years. He helped create the Spider-Man animated series in the mid-1990s. He has written hundreds of comic books and several prose novels.